DON'T EAT DEBT

CARLTON L RILEY SR

DON'T EAT DEBT
(It's bad for our national health)

DON'T EAT DEBT

I would like to dedicate this book to my wife Korin and four kids: Sarita, Kayla, Ashley and Carlton Jr. I love you all more than I have words to express.

Also special thanks to everyone who helped in the development of this book.

CARLTON L RILEY SR

DON'T EAT DEBT

CARLTON L RILEY SR

DON'T EAT DEBT
(It's bad for our national health)
Recipes for a Healthy National Economy with a side of 2008 Crisis and American Monetary History

By Carlton L. Riley Sr.

DON'T EAT DEBT

DON'T EAT DEBT
(It's bad for our national health)
Published by Carlton Riley Sr.
Jacksonville, Florida
(904) 210-7834

This book or parts thereof may not be reproduced in any form, stored in a retrieval system, or transmitted in any form by any means—electronic, mechanical, photocopy, recording or otherwise—without prior written permission of the publisher, except as provided by United States of America copyright law.

Cover design by Carlton L. Riley Sr.

Copyrights © 2012 by Carlton L. Riley Sr.
All rights reserved

Registered in the Library of Congress Pending

First Edition

CARLTON L RILEY SR

DON'T EAT DEBT

CARLTON L RILEY SR

TABLE OF CONTENTS

Introduction..14

1 Can Anyone Read the menu?...................................19

2 The Recession: Over one million pink slips served......29

3 How mortgage back sausages are made.......................37

4 AIG: The white truffle of the recession.........................55

5 American Original Financial Recipe..............................63

6 Recipe for a health Personal Economy.........................83

7 A hungry nation needs to be FED................................91

8 Will that be Cash or Credit?..103

Appendix..110

DON'T EAT DEBT

CARLTON L RILEY SR

DON'T EAT DEBT
(It's bad for our national health)
Recipes for a Healthy National Economy with a side of 2008 Crisis and American Monetary History

By Carlton L. Riley Sr.

DON'T EAT DEBT

INTRODUCTION

Let's put the American monetary system into perspective. The average American citizen knows more about Superman than they know about the American monetary system. The extent of my personal knowledge about the American monetary system was limited to basic common economic sense: I worked, they paid me; I paid my bills and hoped to have money left over for other stuff.

When I wrote a check, I knew I wrote a check, they (receiving party) processed the check and took the money from my account. I never thought about the processing of a check. I have surveyed people from all walks of life. I posed the question, "What do you know about the Federal Reserve System?" This is the bank the American government uses. Most of the people surveyed knew little to nothing of the Federal Reserve System which is a system so important that once it was placed into operation America began the process of weaning our currency off the gold standard. This action had international consequences and a major impact on our economy today.

Despite the FED's importance, the people I interviewed, from corporate executives to sanitation workers, college graduates to IRS agents and even international business executives did not know the slightest thing about the Federal Reserve System and how it relates to their personal financial lives. Prior to the economic crunch of 2008 I knew very little about the Federal Reserve. The more I researched to get a better understanding of circumstances leading into the recession, the more I realized I did not know exactly what tools the FED, Congress and the President had available to resolve the issues. I learned a little about the Federal Reserve in college as to how it related to business but nothing of its connection to personal finance. I could not clearly see the association between the Federal Reserve and the role it played in my personal economy. The more I looked for answers, the more I knew I needed to go back to the beginning of the American financial system to make sense of what I was hearing in the news.

I began writing this book to supply myself and my kids with an understanding of the 2008 crisis as well as provide for them a foundational reference of the economic system. I have found the answers to how American money gets its value, questions of the recessions, FED and our monetary history.

ECONOMICS AND THE FOOD CONNECTION

Once I understood the foundational issues leading to the crisis, I realized its parts are as intertwined as a sausage, and by relating this topic to food it became easier for any non-economist to understand.

The economy is a necessary topic that many seem to avoid talking about unless there is a crisis unlike food which is discussed daily everywhere by everybody. Just like food the economy is necessary for survival. The American economy and crisis is neither scary nor complex once you get a basic understanding. I used a food related chapter titles to make the

DON'T EAT DEBT

information easier to digest and convert into readily accessible knowledge.

The economy should not be an intimidating matter for which only the elite who understand it can benefit and prosper. The financial system is something we have to discuss in order to become and maintain a healthy economic presence in the world today and for future generations. I have made the American monetary system easy to understand so we the citizens can monitor and influence what happens in our country with our money. My life has been changed for the better since gaining this knowledge. Now when I watch the news or hear a news report about the economy it no longer sounds like mumbo-jumbo, (although there is still a lot of rhetoric being communicated), I have a better understanding and now I'm a watchman making a difference starting with the publishing of this book.

By reading and using this information you can make better decisions for yourself and the nation overall.

There is a very simple formula to get the most out of this book:
1. *Start now.*
2. *Use what you have.*
3. *Do what you can.*

I started where I was. I had a desire to understand where the American economy and the crisis was taking us. I started gathering data for what became this book back in 2008.

I used what I had. From my computers, books, magazine articles, videos documentaries, interviewed travelers, internet searching for consistent data and information to see a clearer picture of the crisis and a firm foundation about the money I worked so hard to earn. I used nearly every resource at my disposal to get this information for you to provide a resource to enhance your economic knowledge.

Now I'm doing what I can. Digital or ink print, news programs, blogging, whatever I can to pass this knowledge on to you, so we will never repeat this financial disaster thus creating a worse mess than we are currently experiencing.

It is my sincere desire this book will help you and your families make wiser financial decisions going forward. This is food for your economic soul. Eat it all, Bon-appetite!!!

DON'T EAT DEBT

CHAPTER 1

CAN ANYONE READ THE MENU?

"THE ONLY THING MORE EXPENSIVE THAN EDUCATION IS IGNORANCE." BEN FRANKLIN

I'm not an economist I'm a writer who contributes to the economy. An economist understands numbers, graphs and charts but lacks the wisdom to take into account human nature. I could not tell you how many economists there are in this country but I can tell you there's not nearly enough to provide one on one attention to every American which leads to a dilemma. It was the lack of knowledge on the part of the masses to stop the great recession of 2008. As Ben Franklin said, "the only thing more expensive than education is ignorance." We as a nation are paying the cost of ignorance. Looking back we could have made a difference if we were clear about how the American economy functions.

DON'T EAT DEBT

Let's take a look back before the real estate market crash of 2008. Back when nearly anyone could buy a home with no money down, make a few repairs, beautify the exterior, sell it and repeat this action until they became multimillionaires. Prior to the recession I earned a living as an analyst for CSX railroad. I wasn't rich, but my income stretched further in the past versus these current recessive times. I think back to the days when I stood at the water cooler or the break room complaining about how gas was nearly two dollars per gallon.

Before I purchased my first home in 2003 I was homeless. When I first moved to Florida I leased a four bedroom, two bath home for one year. When the one year lease was over, I remained in the home with my wife and four kids on a month to month agreement. Three months into the second year the owner decided he was moving back to Jacksonville and I had one month to pack up our things and move.

With the housing market in Florida booming it was nearly impossible to find a reasonably priced home in the time frame allotted. It was even harder to close the deal on a home though the average mortgage company was swamped by mounds of new customers. With no home in sight and the month running out, I moved our belongings into a storage unit and moved my family into a hotel. We were taking it one day at a time.

One day while talking to a co-worker I discovered she was in the process of renovating a home converting it into a daycare. She offered to let my family and I move in while it was being renovated and she was getting the necessary paperwork and permits for the daycare. In return I did maintenance work around the center. I searched for a permanent residence. I found a home for sale which allowed us to move in while the loan was being processed, but in the midst of getting approved for a mortgage I was downsized leaving me unemployed. Fortunately for me I was hired at a new company in a similar field. The new company used the same payroll software making it appear as if I had made an internal company transfer *not* a total job change. Despite the challenges I faced we persevered to become home owners, so if you are facing a similar issue the knowledge gained in this book will be a great asset to you. In a later chapter I will give you more insight into my mortgage, but I wanted you to understand I have faced some financial challenges in my life and would never want to position my family nor want to see anyone else go through the same experiences.

More money than homes

I never imagined I would be a part of a recession that was just a hair short of a depression. Most Americans unexpectedly arrived at this financial derailment dazed and confused. But why did we crash? Where were the politicians standing on their soapbox shouting, a recession is coming, a recession is coming? Where were the protesters marching against the establishment to keep America financially safe? Where was the public outcry that caused early Americans to fight for justice? We missed the signs and now we are stuck in a financial rut! Stuck!

Ok, we have the Occupy Wall Street movement. The Occupy Wall Street movement is a people-driven movement that began on September 17, 2011. Initially they did not appear to have any clear objectives, but now it has become an international movement whose goal is a cry for equal distribution of income, bank and government reform to deal with the corruption in politics palpitated by well-funded lobbyists. The movement has spread from Liberty Square in Manhattan's Financial District to

DON'T EAT DEBT

over 100 cities in the United States and actions in over 1,500 cities globally.

I'm glad for the protesters but the truth is had we learned from our past mistakes, we would have collectively seen the crash coming and pushed for changes before the disaster. The media provided warning signs, but we did not understand the writing on the wall. The economist warnings were like financial hieroglyphics. If only Indiana Jones was here to read the economic writing on the wall to stop the crash.

It was President George Washington who said, "It is better to offer no excuse than a bad one." The politicians and Washington power mongers are playing the blame game and making excuses. In this information age we are living in there's no excuse. My goal is to help you understand how we got into this mess and lay a foundation of understanding to provide a stronger and secure financial future.

First we'll take a look at that illusive creature call a recession. Next we'll explore America's monetary history. Then we will look at the key players. Lastly we'll look at a few keys to preserve America's financial strength and power to avoid this type of disaster in the future by improving your personal economy. In this book you will see the effects of not pushing back from the table of economic consumption. This lack of action has left us sick of bail outs and stimulus payments hoping for some type of economic relief like a financial Alka-Seltzer to ease the pain. The pain caused by the crisis feels like a sucker punch to the gut of every American without a lofty tax shelter. It may have knocked us down but we will get up. Why? Because we float like a butterfly and sting like a bee, but we are the greatest nation in history. So lets get started working on a way to cook up a remedy to this mess.

CARLTON L RILEY SR

THE COOKS AND THEIR CODED MENU

I took my daughter shopping for a prom dress in New York City a few years ago. She wanted a unique dress which no one in her high school in Florida could find. As usual we were having a blast in Midtown Manhattan but around lunch time we saw a nice restaurant and decided to get a bite to eat. We found a quaint bistro with a simple black and white décor from the tables to the menu. Standing inside the entrance door waiting for the maître-d I looked at the menu but it did not make sense. The menus were simple black and white menus with numbers written out in word form but random order that appeared to serve no purpose. Just to the right of some sort of dish were numbers; sixteen, twelve, seventy-five, one hundred ten and upward. I told the maître-d I had never seen menus like that and asked what did the numbers represent and he explained how the menu was designed. Once he explained it to me we decided to eat elsewhere. There is an old adage that if you have to ask the prices you can't afford it. That is how I felt every time I heard a news reporter, television announcer, politician and economist talk about the declining economy after the crash and who was to blame. I could see the words and numbers but drawing a clear understanding was impossible due to their presentation. The frustrations were compounded by the endless amount of acronyms being used. With all the fingers being pointed I wanted to ask all of the responsible parties the same question.

DON'T EAT DEBT

The question that permeates in my mind is what the hell were they thinking? The FED, SEC, AIG, Bankers, Hedge Fund managers, investment managers, and anyone else who failed to see the potential dangers of MBS, CDO, CMO and CMO of ABS'? It's like the person speaking is a big baby who picks up a spoon of alphabet soup and expounds in gibberish about their letter combinations. The truth is we have failed to read the road signs leading to the current financial crash.

I had no justified reason for not pushing myself to clearly understand the many voices in government controlling our monetary and fiscal systems. What is your excuse? You have none! We have to educate ourselves now starting with reading and absorbing the information in this book.

While I was pointing a finger at the politicians for the mess I had three other fingers pointing back at myself.

Ben Franklin said, "The only thing more expensive than education is ignorance." During the initial entrance into the 2008 crisis, I listened to the economic analysts, but there were many voices attempting to explain the crisis. My job allows me to interact with people from around the world. Everyone I surveyed from various walks of life seemed unsure of the economist's explanation of the crisis. Translate the following statement spoken by an economist on a public radio program:

> *"Due to the MBS crisis, banks are not issuing commercial papers, so a great many companies are closing their doors for good. AIG defaulted because their CDS had to make some massive payouts due to the decreased values on the properties including CDO and CMO holdings. As the world continues to grapple with fallout from toxic assets which is a key cause of the credit*

crunch, we as a nation are about to see the end of investment banking as we know it."

I haven't heard so many acronyms since I left the military. Granted these are all commonly used acronyms by the media to explain the crisis, the average individual didn't see a complete picture. We can't blame economists for a lack of interest in what they are saying. There are a host of books on the market today talking about our economic crisis but this book is different because it's written in plain English not in a language that only economists understand.

I want to make sure that *we the people* can clearly understand what is going on in the nation's finances and how to make better financial decisions for our businesses, families and country in the years to come.

It was the late actor/singer Will Rogers who said, "An economist's guess is liable to be as good as anybody else's."

I don't mind listening to economists but they tend to speak a language which the average citizen is not familiar with, so we have two options:

(A) We can either hire an interpreter to translate the jargon or

(B) We can learn the language.

Being that you've read this book thus far, it's safe to say you chose *B*. I have learned enough of the language to help make some sense of the financial system. You will not only understand but you'll be able to talk about the statement above with confidence by the time you finish this book.

DON'T EAT DEBT

CARLTON L RILEY SR

DON'T EAT DEBT

CHAPTER 2

THE RECESSION: OVER 1 MILLION PINK SLIPS SERVED

"IN A RECESSION THERE IS NEVER A SHORTAGE OF MONEY IN THE WORLD; IT IS JUST A MATTER OF KNOWING WHERE TO FIND IT THEN SECURE A PORTION FOR YOURSELF." C. L. RILEY SR.

Ask ten people today the definition of a recession and you'll get ten different answers. President Truman said, "A recession is when your neighbor loses his job. A depression is when you lose yours." I have read through page after page of explanations and definitions of a recession, but the answers always vary. I have routinely heard reporters say that we are in a recession. But what exactly is the definition of a recession? When I started researching, no exact definition of a recession could be found.

DON'T EAT DEBT

The responses are usually centered on the speaker's field of expertise or profession. One writer said (to which I totally agree) that the definition of a recession is as hard to define as the word love. The basic definition of a recession is a decline in GDP for two or more consecutive quarters. A drop in the stock market, an increase in unemployment, and a decline in the housing market usually accompany a recession.

An interesting piece of information you need to pay close attention to is the use of GDP and GNP. A basic definition for GDP (gross domestic product) is the total market value of goods and services produced within the borders of a country regardless of the nationality of the producers.

GNP (gross national product) is the total market value of goods and services produced by the residents of a country, even if they do not reside in their home country.

Simply put the GDP is when you add the total market value of goods and services produced within America's borders for legal profit generated by all of the blood, sweat and tears of every American working for three months. You write the Government a check for the money generated and you have our GDP. If you take the GDP and include financial gains of goods and services generated from outside of our borders as a source of income for an American company or individual including investments in foreign markets you would an example of GNP.

My definition of a recession for this book comes from the U.S. Commerce Department's Under Secretary who says a recession is when the GNP (gross national product) falls at least 5% (an example of 5% would mean a drop from $560 billion to $532 billion a difference of $28,000,000,000). This is not the only definition but the one which best fits my research. In terms of who decides if America is in a recession Congress usually relies on a report from the National Bureau of Economic Research also known as NBER before they declare a recession. NBER is a private, nonprofit, nonpartisan research organization dedicated to promoting a greater understanding of how the economy works. NBER was founded in 1920. NBER provides unbiased economic research among public policymakers, business professionals, and the academic community. The NBER organization doesn't need to have two consecutive falling quarters to declare a nation is in a recession.

Though it's rarely talked about during good economic times the word recession is a common part of the business cycle. One thing many economists agree on is the business cycle. The business cycle is a period of economic growth and decline usually over three to four years. The business cycle is a four stage process consisting of expansion, growth, contraction and recession.

A recession in the context of a business cycle is also correction in the market place. In late 2008 we entered into the fourth state of the cycle, which leads us back to the starting point of expansion. The current recession was more severe than most the nation has faced, possibly as serious as the great depression but we will recover. Keep in mind that even in a recession there is never a shortage of money in the world; it is just a matter of knowing where to find it then secure a portion for yourself. During an economic downturn start-up costs are much lower making it a good time to start a business. Kentucky Fried Chicken and Hewlett Packard are two of many companies started during the Great Depression. If you are an entrepreneur you need to make the best of the crisis by providing your service, or product to new markets. With businesses closing

DON'T EAT DEBT

equipment and assets could be purchased for next to nothing. Commercial rents are cheap due to companies going out of business while educated and skilled people are looking for jobs.

According to the Small Business Administration website an estimated 552,600 new employer firms opened for business in 2009.

Also according to the SBA site small firms employed 59.9 million and large firms employed 60.7 million private sector nonfarm workers in 2007. Small business' have a major impact on the nation's bottom line. Help turn someone's status from unemployed to new hire today as you grow financially.

MY STORY

When I financed my first home my wife and I had less than perfect credit so we were offered teaser interest rates. A teaser interest rate is an abnormally low interest. It should have been higher based on our credit score but they had to entice more customers. The rates that lenders offered had a limited initial period (in my case the first two years) in order to entice borrowers to receive adjustable rate mortgages. We were required to pay higher interest rates after the initial period. You may have fallen for that beautiful carrot yourself if you received an A.R.M. My adjustable rate mortgage meant my interest rate on the loan was periodically adjusted based on fluctuations within three percent of the prime interest rate. I watched the market closely because I believed the lie. The lie that millions of other homebuyers like me believed that we would be able to refinance our homes before our interest rate increased.

CARLTON L RILEY SR

As I studied the housing market forecast I began to see financial analysts shared a common consensus. The housing market was oversaturated with overvalued homes being sold to anyone looking to buy. It was this heavy saturation of overvalued homes in real estate markets around the world that became one of the main ingredients of the housing market crash leading to the global recession. No one disputes that the housing market crash was the leading factor which led to the recessions. In a matter of 3½ years I purchased my home for $99,000 and sold it for $151,000. I was fortunate because I sold my home two years prior to the market turning completely sour and I made a fairly good profit, but I did not expect it to end in a recession of this magnitude.

I began to research to get a lucid understanding of how or why the housing crisis in America could lead the rest of the world into an international recession. The more I listened to the news or watched television I noticed everyone sharing their opinion of how we got into the crisis, how long they believed it was going to last and potential ways to get out of the recession before it becomes a depression. A depression is an extended recession.

No one has an absolute answer out of this recession and you won't find it in this publication, but I will provide a list of contributing cooks (responsible politicians, bankers, public servants etc.) that helped to get us to this expensive place called a recession.

During my research I noticed the financial experts (i.e. bankers, stock analysts and economic analysts) words sound like mumbo-jumbo and rhetoric. As I learned more about our overall monetary system their mumbo-jumbo and rhetoric made sense a majority of the time. It is my intention to help

DON'T EAT DEBT

you, my readers, make better sense of what is going on with your money. Most of all I would like for you to read this book twice then locate a financial media source such as CNBC, CNN financial, or Wall Street Journal online etc. to enjoy the knowledge gained from this book and see how it has helped your understanding. As we become better informed citizens, then we as a nation can make better financial decisions. I'm a firm believer in the saying that knowledge is power. If America is going to remain the most powerful nation in the world we will have to make better financial decisions leading to a greater hope and a prosperous future.

We Americans are recovering from this recession as we have every recession that preceded it. As we've done in the past, we as a nation will once again emerge wiser and stronger from this current crisis. It is, after all, *THE AMERICAN WAY*.

CARLTON L RILEY SR

DON'T EAT DEBT

CHAPTER 3

HOW MORTGAGE BACKED SAUSAGES ARE MADE

"IT IS NOT FROM THE BENEVOLENCE OF THE BUTCHER, THE BREWER, OR THE BAKER THAT WE EXPECT OUR DINNER, BUT FROM THEIR REGARD TO THEIR OWN INTEREST." ADAM SMITH

Before we jump right into the recipe for mortgage back sausage there are a few words and descriptions you need to know. Most countries around the world have a form of a central bank. America's central bank is called the Federal Reserve System commonly referred to as the FED.

LET'S GET SOME SAUSAGE, RICE AND GRAVY

The FED is what I call the unofficial fourth branch of the U.S. Government: Judicial, Legislative, Executive and Financial branches. The Fed's job is to regulate our economy. The FED

DON'T EAT DEBT

controls the amount of American currency in circulation at any given time which is why I call them the fourth branch. I will go into more details about the FED in chapter five but we can't look at the process of making mortgage back sausage (I mean Securities) without referencing to the FED. One other item we need to discuss is market bubbles.

A definition of a market bubble is a stock market phenomenon characterized by rapid expansion in a particular sector out of proportion to their basic value. This is followed by a market contraction which is a drastic drop in prices as a massive sell off in that particular sector which is called a market crash.

Another term you need to know is open market. Open market is a term used to describe an unrestricted market with free access by competition of buyers and sellers. In an open market system it is the people conducting business who set the prices for goods and services being conducted and not the government. The Government sets rules to protect consumers conducting business to insure the transactions are being handled in an honest and ethical manner while not imposing restrictions which could hinder market growth.

According to the FED the 1990's was deemed the "longest peacetime economic expansion in our country's history". It was a time when the internet was still in its infancy, entrepreneurs around the world were looking for every conceivable way to make their investment dollars grow. This time period was known as the Dot-Com era.

There was money to be made on the internet. The Dot-Com era gave birth to multiple millionaires and a few billionaires who took their internet based or internet services connected companies' public. Taking a company public meant they began selling shares of their corporations to the general public allowing the investor to be part owners. Some companies provided stock options to their employees during or before the company's initial public offering making them wealthy beyond their dreams once their shares matured meaning after the stock actually began trading on the open market. Money was made online also by providing the infrastructure to support and sustain this growing market. Internet companies sprang up everywhere looking for capital to turn their internet ideas into potential money, money and more money. In early 2001, the Dot-Com bubble burst ending its economic era.

Some investors did not lose all of the money acquired from their internet ventures, but through planning began looking for the next great money making investment. The next great investment came in the form of real estate investing and mortgage insurance.

The real estate market was steadily increasing prior to the 9/11 attacks. In an effort to stabilize American financial markets, after the terrorist attacks, the FED lowered interest rates which helped an already growing housing market pick up momentum. Wall Street Investment brokers seeing the boom in the real estate market began to seriously shop a mortgage product called MBS or mortgage-backed securities.

Mortgage-backed securities are debt obligation (obligation meaning debt entitlements) which represents claims for the securities owner to receive the cash flow from pools of mortgage loans. An easier way to see MBS is it gives the owners of the MBS the right to receive the principal and interest paid on a specific mortgage loan.

DON'T EAT DEBT

Two of the most common types of MBS are CDO and CMO. CDO stands for Collateral Debt Obligations and CMO stands for Collateral Mortgage Obligations. Although they vary slightly they operate the same through a process called securitization.

Before I can explain securitization I have to explain quasi-governmental. Quasi-governmental means supported by the government but managed privately. In terms of the securitization process it means of instead the government personally overseeing the securitization process they outsourced the process to private companies. In the securitization process private entities i.e. (governmental or quasi-governmental individuals or groups) purchased mortgage loans from banks, mortgage companies and other loan originators and assembled these loans into pools. The private entity, governmental, or quasi-governmental then issues securities that represent claims on the principal and interest payments made by the borrowers on the loans in the pool. For some investors, MBS is a way to enter into the real estate market without having the hassle of locating and selling properties for profits. The process of converting an individual mortgage to becoming a Mortgage-backed security has to transition between two types of banks, Commercial and Investment banks. I will give more details of the original bank split in the next chapter, "America's Monetary History".

COMMERCIAL BANKS

The homebuyer generally receives financing from Commercial banks, mortgage companies and other money lenders. Commercial banks are banks that take deposits for checking and savings accounts from consumers. Commercial banks are regulated by the Federal Reserve who also oversees the Federal

Deposit Insurance Corporation (FDIC) which provides insurance for depositors in case the bank runs into liquidity issues. Credit Unions are regulated by the National Credit Union Administration (NCUA).

Successful banks and credit unions must be prepared with a substantial cash reserve for withdrawals at anytime. In other words they must remain liquid. Liquidity is the ability of a financial institution to meet its financial commitments without incurring unacceptable losses. The FDIC was created to prevent banks from failing if a high percentage of their accountholders attempt to withdraw their money. Commercial banks have to retain a portion of their deposit to cover customer requests to withdraw their funds at a moment's notice. That is essentially why the FED is called the Federal **Reserve** Bank. It is where the banks keep their reserves. When the percentage of customers withdrawing their funds exceeds a bank's ability to procure the funds in a timely manner then the FDIC covers the needed funds.

The FDIC is an independent agency created by Congress to guarantee the safety of bank deposits—by insuring deposit balances up to predetermined amounts. Currently, FDIC insures each depositor up to $250,000 per insured bank. FDIC does not insure money invested in stocks, bonds, mutual funds, life insurance policies, annuities or municipal securities. Congress specifies the insurance limits of FDIC.

If your bank defaults, then the FDIC will payout for lost money from your savings or checking but not for financial instruments such as the MBS.

Think of it this way. Let's say checking and savings accounts are like rice, a staple for sustaining life, then a bond is like gravy. Gravy isn't a staple, but it generally makes the rice taste

DON'T EAT DEBT

better. A bond isn't money you labored for it's an investment that leverages the works of others paying you interest and enhances your income. The FDIC mainly covers deposit accounts which are usually money used to sustain a household. So what is a bond? I'm glad you asked!

A bond is essentially a loan to a government, municipality, corporation, federal agency or other entity similar to an I.O.U., granted for a certain period of time at a fixed interest rate. When the bond matures or comes due the issuer pays a specified rate of the face value of the bond. So if a financial institution is heavy in debt because homeowners default on their mortgages, the FDIC covers the bank's losses on defaulted bank insured mortgages (the rice) but not on Mortgage Backed Securities (the gravy) because they are financial instruments.

The FDIC's primary objective is to insure bank deposits and reduce the economic disruptions caused by bank failures. Once the home buyer completes the closing process the loans goes back to the commercial bank or mortgage lender to service or to be sold.

Once the mortgage paperwork is complete the Commercial banks (or other mortgage lender) process the loans; they bundle similar mortgage loans together which they submit to a MBS dealer/issuer for securitization.

A CLOSER LOOK AT THE GRAVY

When a person takes out a mortgage they are the Mortgagor. A mortgage in simple terms is when an individual or company borrows money to purchase land commonly referred to as real estate property. When the Mortgagor signs a mortgage they are granting the lender a stake in the property, which allows them to lend the funds with an accurate assessment of risk. The mortgagor provides the lender with a guarantee for the full repayment of the loan. Securitization is when all of the individual mortgages are bundled together into a mortgage pool, which is held in trust as the collateral for the MBS.

In summary the mortgagor makes an agreement to have the bank issue them credit for the purposes of acquiring a home. The mortgagor (the person who received the mortgage loan) signs an agreement stating if they don't make their payments, the bank can have the property. The commercial bank bundled the mortgages together through the securitization process converting a random group of mortgages into a trust and sells the mortgages and the payments from the mortgages to a secondary mortgage markets in a new form of money producing product known as *mortgage backed securities.*

For simplicity sake let's think of Fannie Mac and Sally Mae as the loan issuers' rich aunts and uncles. They make sure the mortgage backed securities buyer receives their money if the housing market crash. Fannie Mac and Sally Mae are also quasi-governmental organizations. Again, quasi-governmental means supported by the government but managed privately. Once the pools are securitized, the dealer/issuer then sells the MBS to institutional and individual investors. The lender who delivered the mortgages for securitization usually continues to service the loans. By servicing the loans I'm referring to processing payments, maintaining the property owner's financial status and reporting the homebuyer's payment history to a credit bureau.   At the writing of this book four years into the crisis the government has taken control of the mortgage giant to prevent it from failing, but Fannie Mae is still one of the largest private corporations in America.

DON'T EAT DEBT

INVESTMENT BANK

One such institution that purchased MBS and the second bank in this formula for disaster is the Investment bank. Investment banks are regulated by the Securities & Exchange Commission or as it is commonly call the SEC. Investment banks help companies raise capital for growth and expansion. MBS are one of the tools Investment banks use to help companies raise quick capital. The Investment banker purchases MBS products such as Collateral Mortgage Obligations, then divides them into tranches and sells the tranches to investors. Tranches are the result of MBS after they are divided into parts or slices. Depending on the level of risk an investor is willing to take; various tranches are paid in a specific order. Payout is based on the mortgage maturity ranging from one, two, and five years up to but not limited to 20-year maturities. Senior tranches get paid first to allow risk-averse investors who might need short term cash flow now. Risk-loving investors take the greatest risk of the tranches and receive a higher return to meet their cash flow needs in the future.

During the Real-Estate market bubble, tens of thousands of CMO/CDO MBS were sold to money managers, pension funds, trust departments, hedge fund managers, insurance companies, commercial banks, securities dealers, major corporations, and private investors around the world.

Initially the American and international housing markets and economies were going strong. MBS were great investments and considered as safe as Treasury bonds also called T-Bonds. Treasury bonds or notes as they are called are American debt notes sold to buyers with the promise that the government will pay the buyer back with interest after a set period of time commonly referred to as maturity date.

Being that America has never failed to pay its debts, T-Bonds are considered internationally as a safe investment. But MBS were a really different beast.

As the real estate market grew, lending standards became lackadaisical. The underwriting or qualifying of loans for people with a less than desirable credit rating increased leading the way to what economists called sub-prime lending. The difference between prime interest rates and subprime interest rates is simple. A Prime interest rate is the rate of interest charged to people with excellent credit. Sub-Prime lending is the process of providing loans at a higher interest rate for persons with blemished or limited credit histories. They charge a higher interest rate to compensate for their increased credit risk.

As the housing bubble was developing, a CNN report stated that nearly half of the loans made in 2006 were sub-prime loans. Sub-prime lending gained momentum from 2004 to 2007 creating a plethora of risk laden loans which banks continued to bundle and sell these sub-prime loans to MBS investors.

Since neither the Commercial nor the Investment banks were planning to hold on to the potentially toxic loans, they willingly took greater risks. Both the FED and the SEC should have sounded the alarm and took actions to detour Commercial and Investment banks from taking on such an unusual amount of risk but little was done. With no limits in sight to hinder growth in the housing sector of America's economy, the business cycle went into full swing. MBS could be found in portfolios around the world. From central banks to private retirement accounts and hedge funds, Mortgage Backed Securities seemed to be the

DON'T EAT DEBT

sure investment to own. With the housing industry on the rise the law of supply and demand took its natural course.

HOW TO COOK A GOOSE: LAW OF SUPPLY AND DEMAND IN THE HOUSING SECTOR

The business cycle is a process of economic growth and decline. There are four stages in a business cycle: expansion, growth, contraction and recession. The business cycle reflects the predictable changes and fluctuations that an economy goes through on a regular basis, over a long period of time. The law of supply and demand states that as demand increases the price goes up which attracts new suppliers who increase supplies thus providing stability to the price of the goods or services. The law of supply and demand in the case of the housing market went like this:

CARLTON L RILEY SR

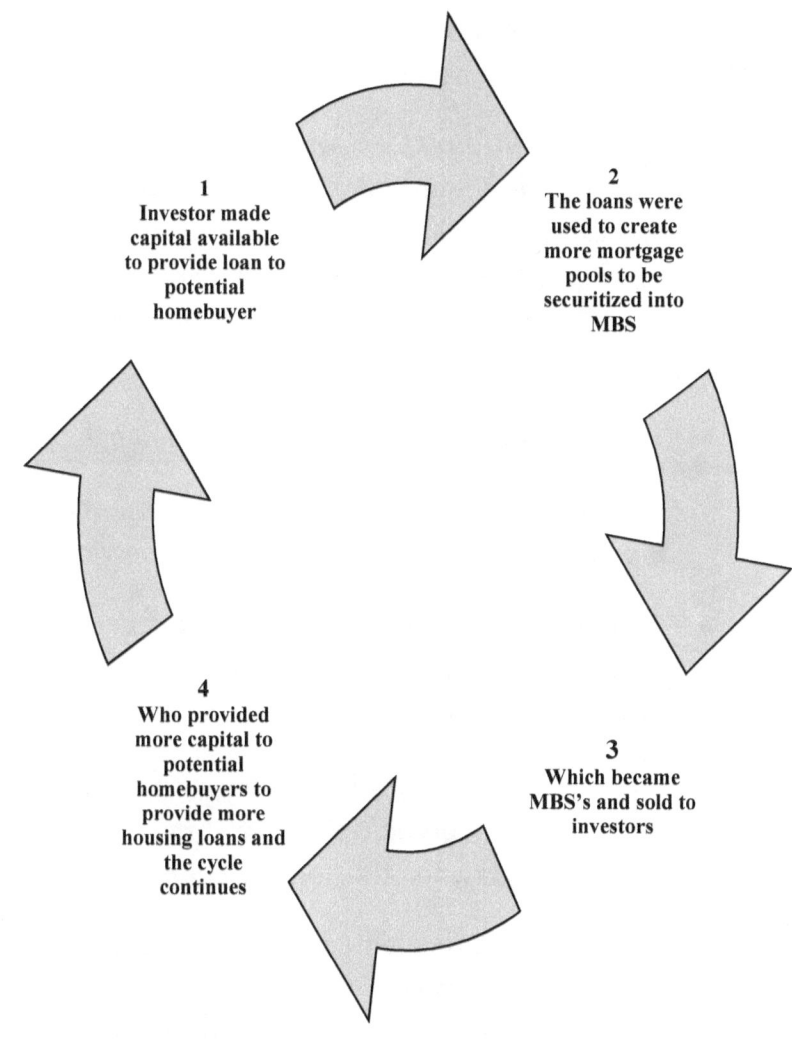

Due to the continual growing housing markets, real estate prices continued to grow at a momentous pace due largely to the number of people in the market for homes. Property values sky rocketed due to the many housing developments being built with adequate funding being provided by lending

DON'T EAT DEBT

institutions with slack lending practices making it possible to sell the homes almost as fast as they were being built.

I bought an ARM mortgage which developers used teaser rates to entice sub-prime homebuyers into their multimillion dollar establishments. The lending institutions steadily churned out MBS to meet the demand of a continuously growing market. MBS appeared to create a triumphant product for everyone involved:

- The home buyer received money for a home

- Lender resold the mortgage to investors in the second mortgage market while getting paid to service the loans.

- Fannie Mae and Freddie Mac continued to grow while they insured more mortgage notes and also received payment for securitized mortgages

- Investors made money from the tranches and received payments from Credit Default Swaps which is insurance for MBS if and when the housing bubble bursts.

The housing market needed correction. It continued to grow at an unsustainable rate. Please keep in mind that the mortgage market is predominantly a credit based system with little to no actual cash transaction.

A Greedy Chef will always starve the Customers

All was well as long as the job market was strong, consumer spending was up and credit markets flowed freely. A greedy chef I like to call G.R.E.G. (Greed Repulsive Energy Giants) approached the economic kitchen. G.R.E.G. showed up with a shiny spoon and said "American disposable income! Get in my belly." As G.R.E.G. caused the fuels prices to soar, G.R.E.G. began to eat up the disposable income of American consumers which in turn hurt retail businesses.

I personally had to start making seemingly small concessions to compensate for the rising fuel costs. At first it was eat at home a little more or be more conservative on the utilities around the house. Next as fuel costs continued to rise, it was decrease my Starbucks trips to maybe three times per week (which a lot harder than it sounds) from five. As the fuel prices started to deeply affect consumers (such as myself) we had to make stern budget choices to compensate for the economic repercussions of overpriced fuel.

In a survey conducted by the National Small Business Association, 28% of the small businesses surveyed in 2006 had to increase the prices they charged customers due to rising fuel costs.

Fuel costs grew to the point that companies started laying people off. It was the third stage of the business cycle called contraction also called a shrinking market.

Contraction is the law of supply and demand in reverse. As demand decreases the price goes down which causes the number of suppliers to decrease the supply thus creating instability to the price of the goods or services. A contraction should not be mistaken as a bear market which is discussed in a later chapter. A contraction is a short term correction in the market.

As the job market worsened, people had to make the harder choices such as pay their mortgage or buy food? In most cases food prevailed. With money issues and unemployment on the rise, homeowners in all classes went into default.

DON'T EAT DEBT

MBS value began to lose momentum as sub-prime borrowers began to default on their mortgages. As the economy worsened the credit market began to tighten its belt and slowing down credit lending especially commercial paper for day to day business operation which was essential for some company's survival.

Commercial paper is an unsecured, line of credit businesses use typically for financing of accounts receivable, inventories and meeting short-term liabilities. The primary mortgage market is based on property being used as collateral, but the resources provided by commercial paper are needed to help finance business daily operations. In our credit laden economy there is a simple rule that governs most businesses: *no credit, no business*.

When I began writing this book I worked as a Senior Quality Analyst for SourceOne Healthcare Technologies which was the largest medical equipment and supplies provider in America. It was created by combining the number one and two companies in their industry.

Before the merger of the companies, the radiology side of the company made the bulk of its income at the end of the year thus requiring outside funds to operate for the first three quarters of the year. The parent company funded us on the front end and the radiology company settled its debt the fourth quarter as well as turned a profit. Some companies aren't fortunate enough to have a private backer.

The commercial paper market works like a credit card for big companies. Commercial paper was traded in the form of money market mutual funds and considered safe until large well-respected companies started failing and the people who had held these bonds actually lost money. Maturities on commercial paper rarely range any longer than eight months. As the companies started going under, the pool of lenders dried up. It only added to the decline in our GDP. The credit issues only snow balled as the MBS continued to default.

A QUICK RECIPE REVIEW

Prior to the 9/11 attacks, the government made it easier for every American to achieve the dream of home ownership. Recovering from the worse attack on American soil, we united as a nation sending the message to our attacker that these colors (American flag) don't run. One of the objectives of the attack was to destabilize America's economy. The FED lowered interest rates to stabilize America's financial markets. The FDIC, whose primary objective is to insure bank deposits and reduce the economic disruptions, raised payout for each deposited accounts from $100,000 to $250,000 per depositor account.

With the economy stabilized, when internet dot-com bubble busted and the real estate market became the new money making star on the rise. Then entered the commercial and investment firms providing home loans to all whom desired to purchase or invest in the housing market. Homes were sold. Loans issued. Commercial banks bundled mortgage loans in the same manner Midwest farmers bundled wheat but the banks bundled mortgages. MBS' are mortgages bundle together in a trust and sold as securities on the secondary mortgage market. The owners of the MBS are entitled to the cash flows from pools of mortgage loans using the mortgaged homes as collateral. With so much credit available for property purchase the real estate market soared to unsustainable heights before crashing taking the credit markets with it. All was well until

DON'T EAT DEBT

rising fuel cost caused consumers to make financial choices to offset increasing costs.

Eventually many Americans could not afford to sustain their living standards as the cost of living increased and incomes decreased as companies went under. Borrowers began to default on their loans. MBS lost value. Lenders began to pull back the reins on credit, starving companies of much needed commercial paper for day to day operations. For some hope was lost. Fearing the housing market bubble would burst and to protect their portfolios some investors took out insurance for protection. Some of the MBS owners and sellers bought Credit Default Swaps which are commonly referred to as CDS'. CDS' protect against failure among their investments. In the case of MBS, Credit Default Swaps are insurance policies to protect MBS owners if their CDO/CMO loses value or homebuyers default on their loans. AIG was the largest seller of CDS' in the world. The final result, we're in a recession.

CARLTON L RILEY SR

DON'T EAT DEBT

CHAPTER 4
AIG: THE WHITE TRUFFLE OF THE RECESSION

"GOVERNMENT'S VIEW OF THE ECONOMY COULD BE SUMMED UP IN A FEW SHORT PHRASES: IF IT MOVES, TAX IT. IF IT KEEPS MOVING, REGULATE IT. AND IF IT STOPS MOVING, SUBSIDIZE IT."
                                            RONALD REAGAN

In this recipe for financial disaster I have to compare AIG to the white truffle mushroom. In a Time Magazine article online dated Oct. 20, 2010, there was a 1.6 pound white truffle mushroom which sold for $150,000 in 2009. Like this mushroom, AIG cost the American tax payers a heck of a lot of money. Besides its enormous price tag, the white truffle mushroom and AIG debt share one more common connection: they were both foraged by special pigs. The American International Group (AIG) was a major seller of credit default swaps. AIG sold credit default swaps (or CDS which is basically insured debt) to collateral debt obligations/collateral mortgage obligations owners ranging from international central banks to private retirement managers. During the real-estate market excessive growth, insurance giant AIG entered into the 60-70 trillion dollar markets. AIG was seemly the largest seller of CDO/CMO insurance in the world.

Credit default swaps are a type of derivative. Derivatives are financial instrument whose value is based on the value of another financial instrument. In this case the financial instrument is mortgaged payments. In the case of AIG the CDS is a type of insurance policy to protect mortgage backed securities owners if their investment lost value or property owners defaulted on their loans. AIG acted on the massive quantity of money being made in the housing sector of the market. AIG began selling CDS' to mortgage-backed security owners.

AIG was not the only issuer of credit default swaps. Credit default swaps were issued by other banks and hedge fund providers because it was quicker and easier to buy and sell CDS contracts rather than buying and selling actual bonds which the CDS protects. Traditionally, bond issuers seldom go bankrupt which is the reason why they were so popular with AIG, banks and hedge fund providers. These entities made a fortune selling CDS, keeping the premium, and rarely paying out anything. Numerous CDS were sold as insurance to cover those risky financial tools that helped perpetuate the housing crisis.

Most banks and hedge funds managers that sold mortgage backed securities also bought credit default swaps to protect themselves in the event their MBS bonds defaulted. Although MBS seemed very unlikely to crash, they knew they would need continuous incoming revenue to make CDS payouts. Due to a lack of wisdom or greedy executives on the part of AIG, they only sold Credit Default Swaps to clients but failed to purchase insurance for their own MBS. AIG managers failed to pay close attention to the fact that CDS protected product was unlike the typical insurance policies where you could expect predictable trends, but bundled MBS bonds differ. With insurance policies there is a low correlation between insurance causing events and customer payouts.

Here is an example using auto insurance: If one person gets into car accident it is unlikely that every policy holder would get into an accident at the same time causing major payouts at once. With bonds once a specific type of bond starts defaulting, other of the same are more likely to default at an exponential rate.

When mortgage-backed securities and collateralized debt obligations began to default, AIG was making payouts with no CDS premium payment revenue coming in to supplement the losses. It is estimated that AIG wrote more than $440 billion in Credit default swaps. If facing that huge amount of debt was not enough trouble, AIG's credit rating was lowered by multiple credit-rating agencies who declared they had little confidence in AIG's ability to pay its debts. I guess that is the price for being a greedy insurance salesmen. In all honesty I don't feel AIG's greed was reason enough for the American tax payers via the US government to bail them out, but there is more to the story.

AIG is arguably the largest commercial and industrial insurer in the nation or possibly the world. AIG provided CDS protection to Banks all over the world including a few of the foreign central banks of major countries. If AIG was allowed to fail or default on its policies central banks would have lost their protection of the risky bonds. AIG coverage caused trillions of banks dollars to suddenly be at risk. It could've cost the other banks billions of dollars to find another insurance company to replace the AIG coverage. In the end one source said that the

DON'T EAT DEBT

credit default swaps market dwarfed the losses associated with subprime mortgage-backed securities.

As you will see in the section on the *American Monetary System* banks borrow money from other banks. If banks fail to repay other banks they could stop loaning money to each other causing an international freeze of credit much like we are seeing in America today as it spreads to the rest of the world all courtesy of AIG.

LET'S MAKE MORTGAGE BACKED SAUSAGES IN A WHITE TRUFFLE SAUCE

Now that you have the foundational understanding of the various tools used to get into the crisis let's put it all together for a practical view.

Let's say mortgage backed securities in the form of collateral mortgage obligations and collateralized debt obligations are types of IOU's. Mr. Homebuyer signs an IOU to a commercial bank and tells them we will pay you xxx amount of dollars for the next 30 years until the loan is paid off. If you don't pay your mortgage loan per your agreement the banker can take your house and keep the money you have already paid. Now this process happens repeatedly by Mr. Commercial Banker.

Now Mr. Commercial Banker takes one hundred of these IOU's to his friend the Loan Butcher and tells him I will sell you one hundred IOU's for xxx amount of dollars and you can collect the interest and principal payments based on the terms I negotiated with Mr. Homebuyer. The Loan Butcher buys the 100 mortgage IOU's and mixes them together into a mortgage sausage and cuts them into slices called tranches and sells them to his friend Mr. Investment Banker. Mr. Investment Banker sells his MBS or Mortgage Backed Sausages (oops!) securities to multiple investors. That is a simplified example of how an MBS works.

To complicate the matter, some of the loans included in an investor's mortgage backed securities have possibly changed banks several times before they reached his MBS which makes it hard for Mr. Homebuyer to actually know who has his mortgage.

Today one of the main challenges facing homebuyer's whose homes are in foreclosure is trying to determine who owns their loans and the value of the property involved: is it the original lending institution the MBS mediator or the MBS owner? These are the reasons the media calls the foreclosed properties involved in MBS trouble, Toxic Assets. Before the security owner can determine the value of the each security, they must first determine which bank or creditor actually has legal right to the property and what it worth since home prices have fallen and the real estate bubble burst.

Let's put this new knowledge in motion. The crisis reporting should be more understandable simply by helping you to see somewhat in an orderly manner, how we got into this mess. The terminology is not so hard to understand anymore. The sting of the crisis should not burn as bad, nor the fear that the American economy will never recover as stated by the naysayers, media and analysts. We've overcome the crisis but are still working to recover.

A wise man once told me where fear is - bondage soon follows. After reading the first chapter we now know the word "recession" has continued to lead the media though the crisis is over. This is simply because by human nature most people fear the unknown. By keeping people uncertain of our financial future searching for answers to the recession it will continue to sell in the media.

DON'T EAT DEBT

As I conclude this chapter, other than a lack of action from the masses to foresee the crisis, it was the greed of people through the use of mortgage-backed securities, collateralized debt obligations and collateralized mortgage obligations that helped to create the second greatest financial crisis in America's young history while simultaneously causing an international recession.

The government parties such as the FED, SEC, Treasury and Congress involved in watching over the financial markets and their lack of effective action were also as guilty as Wall Street.

We as American citizens must learn from this crisis and teach our kids about it so that they will never experience this issue again in their adult lives. Take a moment and talk with your children or loved ones about the crisis to see how much they understand, then buy them a copy of this book so that they too can get a better understanding of the 2008 crisis and avoid the pitfall themselves.

AUTHOR'S NOTE: Before you continue reading this book it is important for you to understand that although there are still people against America's current financial system just as there were at the founding of this nation, it's not my intent to sway anyone to a particular side. My purpose in writing this book is to simply inform you of our financial system. It is my intention to help you better understand our financial system and to make wiser financial decisions. I want to help you understand the jargon used by the various media in reporting our economic status. I would like to encourage you to continue seeking sources to improve your financial IQ. I assure you this knowledge will serve you well for a lifetime.

CARLTON L RILEY SR

DON'T EAT DEBT

CHAPTER 5

AMERICA'S ORIGINAL FINANCIAL RECIPE: MAKING AMERICAN MONETARY SOUP

"IT IS WELL ENOUGH THAT PEOPLE OF THE NATION DO NOT UNDERSTAND OUR BANKING AND MONETARY SYSTEM, FOR IF THEY DID, I BELIEVE THERE WOULD BE A REVOLUTION BEFORE TOMORROW MORNING." HENRY FORD

Those words were spoken by Henry Ford, a man who graduated from Goldsmith, Bryant & Stratton Business College in Detroit. He was an accounting student who did not believe in accountants. His understanding of our monetary system afforded him the ability to become one of the richest men of his time without ever having his company audited. So the quote above was made with the understanding of how the banking and monetary system worked and his words still ring true today. Upon completion of this chapter ask someone if they know what gives the American dollar its value. You will be

DON'T EAT DEBT

surprised at the responses you get. Our ignorance is costing us millions of dollars per day that we can't afford to lose. Let's learn from our past mistakes now, so that we will not carry them into our future.

LET'S COOK

Currency in America started with the Massachusetts Bay Colony back in 1690 and the other colonies followed suit. For years England put restrictions on the colonists money until 1764 when they outlawed Colonial paper money altogether.

It was not until 1776 that the Continental Congress printed paper money known as "continentals" as a means to finance the American Revolution. It was a pseudo fiat currency. Fiat money is a currency authorized by a government as legal tender. Most established governments during that time had some form of species (coined money) as currency such as gold bullions and coins made of silver or gold. The "continentals" were backed according to the San Francisco Federal Reserve by the "anticipation" of tax revenues from the soon to be independent Nation of America.

The "continentals" were printed in such a quantity during the American Revolution that it led to hyperinflation causing people to lose hope in the notes. As the founding fathers worked to establish a new government, they charted the Bank of North America in Philadelphia to support the newly formed nation's financial operation. The first National Bank was established in 1781. A few years later they established the dollar as America's Fiat monetary unit. Its name was derived from the Spanish silver dolar.

The Spanish silver dolar was considered the most popular form of species because it was cut into eight equal parts of silver. The silver dolar was also the primary form of payment as our new nation struggled toward establishing a more perfect union. British money was hard to find but the Spanish dolar was based on an established measure of weighted silver but America established its own value using pieces of ten. When America began producing the dollar it gave way to the rhymes "2 bits, 4 bits, 6 bits, a dollar" which they are describing 25 cents, 50 cents, 75 cents, a dollar. At the time we did not have a dime. It is believed that the American dollar sign was derived from the initials of the *U*nited *S*tates. If you lay a capital "U" over a capital "S" then drop the lower part of the "U", you end up with is a version of the dollar symbol with two strokes.

The founding fathers worked hard to establish a solid financial system. They wanted to get our government off to a good start. Alexander Hamilton, President George Washington's former military aide was appointed the first Secretary of the Treasury. Famed actor Will Rogers said, "Alexander Hamilton started the U.S. Treasury with nothing, and that was the closest our country has ever been to being even." At the urging of Alexander Hamilton in 1791 America made its first attempt at establishing a national banking system.

In 1792 Congress established the First Bank of the United States based on a twenty year charter and also signed the Coinage act to establish the US Mint. The law established our official monetary system. It set denominations for coins granting specific values to gold, silver and copper coins. The First Bank of the United States was the largest corporation in America at the time but many citizens did not welcome it for fear of the influential power it posed. The belief was he who controls the money controls the nation. Bankers were believed to be no more trustworthy than politicians. At the end of its twenty year charter after much debating over the nation's need for a central bank, Congress in conjunction with proponents

DON'T EAT DEBT

against the bank pushed for dissolving the bank's charter and won by one vote. The First Bank of the United States was closed. Five years later Congress approved a charter for a Second Bank of the United States.

President Andrew Jackson expressed his reservations about a national banking system. President Jackson said,

> *"It is to be regretted that the rich and powerful too often bend the acts of government to their selfish purposes. Distinctions in society will always exist under every just government. Equality of talents, of education, or of wealth cannot be produced by human institutions. In the full enjoyment of the gifts of Heaven and the fruits of superior industry, economy, and virtue, every man is equally entitled to protection by law; but when the laws undertake to add to these natural and just advantages artificial distinctions, to grant titles, gratuities, and exclusive privileges, to make the rich richer and the potent more powerful, the humble members of society- the farmers, mechanics, and laborers-who have neither the time nor the means of securing like favors to themselves, have a right to complain of the injustice of their Government. There are no necessary evils in government. Its evils exist only in its abuses. If it would confine itself to equal protection, and as Heaven does its rain, shower its favors alike on the high and the low, the rich and the poor, it would be an unqualified blessing."*

Congress allowed the charter to expire in 1836. After 1836 America tried a different approach to banking. State-chartered and uncharted banks started issuing their own notes but unlike the continental's currency, the new notes were not a fiat currency and where redeemable in gold or coined money. This time period was known as the Free Banking Era because the banks were free and not subject to a Government bank. To enhance commerce, banks began to demand deposit which is a common practice today as part of our commercial banks. With all the various currencies being exchanged for goods and services, the New York Clearinghouse Association was established to settle accounts and exchange checks.

In 1861 the United States Treasury Department began the process of issuing paper currency. American money received the nickname "greenback" because of the green color. Since the founding of America's monetary system counterfeiters have been looking for a way to counterfeit American currency. The US Treasury added fine-line engraving, a Treasury seal, engraved signatures and intricate geometric lathe work patterns and features to prevent counterfeiting. Initially each American dollar was created by hand, but on August 29, 1862 a workshop was built and became the first location for the Bureau of Engraving and Printing. They printed security documents, currency, revenue stamps and government bonds, notes and Treasury bills also call obligations. America transitioned into a new era.

A little side note: in 1739 Benjamin Franklin created a process of adding raised impression patterns he cast from leaves when printing colonial bills. It was such a unique process as an anti-counterfeiting process it took centuries before the process was understood.

The free banking era turned into the National Banking era after the National Banking Act was signed into law. The

DON'T EAT DEBT

National Banking Act was passed in 1863 during the Civil War. This act established a national banking system overseen by the U.S. Treasury who was also responsible for the establishing and regulating of "national" banks. The National banks were authorized to issue national currency notes that were backed by US government bonds. In an effort to create a uniform currency, (one national currency opposed to individual state currencies) Congress taxed State Bank Notes only, excluding the National Bank Notes. The taxes did little to detour the state banks from printing their own notes.

From 1877 until today the Bureau of Engraving and Printing is the sole producer of currency for the United States. It's still a part of the Treasury Department.

Fast forward to 2012 and you will see that America's currency is currently backed by Treasury bonds and other financial instruments which in theory depend on future taxes to repay the holders just as early America did with the continentals. I pray we don't get the same results.

BAD INGREDIENTS COULD RUIN A GOOD RECIPE

By the end of the National Banking era America had over 30,000 diverse currencies in circulation. During the Civil war nearly one third of the currency in circulation was counterfeit including the National currency.

Counterfeiting became a major issue for the U. S. Government. On July 5, 1865 the Secret Service was created under the Treasury Department to suppress counterfeiters in America. The counterfeiter's efforts were destroying the public's confidence in the Nation's currency. When public confidence is low then spending decreases and the dollar loses value. The Secret Service was the only law office at the time that had complete national jurisdiction which is the reason they later became responsible for the protection of the president. The Secret Service was under the Treasury Department from 1865 to 2001. After 9/11 the Secret Service was placed under the Department of Homeland Security but catching counterfeiters is part of their mission.

In terms of issues caused by counterfeit bills aside from being illegal is they cause inflation and destabilize the economy. Even though there are no real commodities backing our currency, the FED is aware of the money in circulation which it uses to manage inflation. When the FED injects more money into the economy, it drops the value of money in circulation until bonds are sold to insure it value. When money is placed into circulation not introduced by the FED, it undermines bond system which buys and sells US bonds (debt) to other central banks around the world including private investors who could afford to make the purchase. Unauthorized money in circulation weakens the dollar value being there are no bonds to uphold its value.

BACK TO SOUP MAKING

The National Banking Act helped stabilize currency for our growing nation, but people were still skeptical with the banking system. The United States treasury was operating on the gold standard which meant for every financial note America printed the government had gold reserves to back it. By law the government could not print any money that exceeded the correct percentage it represented. We suspended the gold standard practice to finance the Civil war but returned to it shortly after the war was ended.

DON'T EAT DEBT

American currency at that time could be redeemed for its gold or silver value that was held in various banks. The government provided what was called the gold window. Customers at the time could redeem their currency gold notes (predecessor to the Federal Reserve notes we now use) for the actual gold it represented.

For America, being on the gold standard was good for the long term economics because it stabilized our currency and long term interest rates. One of the problems American government encountered while being on the gold standard was the Treasury Department wasn't able to print extra money except in extreme emergencies such as times of war.

The ability to print money as needed is called elastic currency. During domestic disturbances such as bank panics the nation had to find another means to restore consumer confidence. It is consumer confidence that keeps our currency flowing from purse to purchase which was then and still today the way we establish the dollar true value. The job of Government is to keep money changers around the world economically confident in the American dollar.

BANK PANIC: CAUSE OF THE FLAT ECONOMIC SOUFFLÉ

Bank panics sometimes arose when bank customers tried to redeem their gold notes for gold during the holidays and some banks did not have enough gold on hand to meet customer demands. Bank panics often led to run on banks. A run on a bank meant a large number of customers would attempt to withdraw all of their funds from a bank at once. The banker seeing he did not have enough funds in the vault to meet customer demand, would have to close the doors of the bank until he got more money transferred from another bank. When customers discovered a banker refused to allow its customer to withdraw their money, this caused a panic which sometimes turned into a riot.

Run on the banks were common during the late 1800's which left the American economy unstable even triggering economic depression such as the depression of 1893. With no real economic support system in place, America relied on finance mogul J. P. Morgan to pull the nation out of that depression. The government called upon J. P. Morgan again in the early 1900s to ease the nation's financial tensions in the recession of 1907.

Although the American banking system had progressed a long way from 1775 to 1900 the system still needed a lot of work. By 1907 American citizens were asking for a central banking authority to ensure a healthy banking system and create an elastic currency.

With repetition being a key in learning I want to restate that elastic currency means the government has the ability to increase or the decrease the amount of currency in circulation to keep the national economy moving in a healthy direction. Elastic currency was created as a tool to manage inflation and possibly avoid recessions by making sure prices did not climb or drop quickly.

It was clear by 1908 that America needed to create a better banking system. Senator Nelson Aldrich spearheaded the Aldrich-Vreeland Act of 1908 as an immediate response to the panic of 1907. The act allowed the treasury to provide emergency currency during crisis, while working on a long term solution for our national banking issues. Opponents against the

DON'T EAT DEBT

Aldrich-Vreeland Act argued against the bill for fear of the power gained by a central banking system ran by the political powers of the day. Thomas Jefferson said, "Banking establishments are more dangerous than standing armies." The same sentiment was expressed by President Wilson.

In 1912 President Woodrow Wilson ended the Aldrich's banker-controlled plan. President Wilson being limited in his knowledge of financial and banking issues solicited the advice of a fellow politician, Representative Carter Glass and economics professor H. Parker Willis for a solution. The solution came in the form of a decentralized central banking system ran by both government elected officials and non-governmental employees. The concept became America's version of a central bank. The signing of the Federal Reserve Act by President Woodrow Wilson is a classic example of comprise that balanced a decentralized central bank with the same competing interest of privates banks.

On December 23, 1913 President Woodrow Wilson signed the Federal Reserve Act into law. Although its role has been expanding since it was originally created, it is still the very system that governs our monetary policies today.

As you read this keep in mind that this is the history of America's financial system that does not change with politicians, election, and judicial legislation. This is some of the most important history you will learn because it governs our economic future.

The initial design for the FED was to answer the S.O.S call sent out by the American citizens for bank reform. The goals of the Federal Reserve Act were to *S*tabilize, *O*rganize and *S*tandardize the banking system. It was designed to ensure banks could honor withdrawals for customers wanting their money while also establishing public confidence in the United States banking system and provide a stable economy. The Federal Reserve Act also provided the tools needed for elastic currency. Our national currency went from gold or silver certificates to Federal Reserve Notes.

The mission of the FED was to provide the nation with a flexible and safer financial system not governable by mainline politics. To avoid the original issues of the First and Second Banks of the United States the Federal Reserve Act developed a regional banking system. It was designed as a public and private structure. The FED has seven governors appointed by the President. They are called the public sectors because they are appointed to serve as the voice of the people in their region. The seven governors are responsible for overseeing the twelve reserve banks and also have smaller reserve branch banks around the country. The twelve regional banks* each have a president from the private sector and a board of directors selected from various walks of life from bankers to farmers. *See bank list in appendix

The FED regional offices were opened by November 16, 1914 just as World War I was erupting in Europe. With the FED in place America used the power of elastic currency to aid in the flow of trade goods to Europe. We were also able to finance ourselves after we entered World War I in 1917 due to the stable leadership of the FED.

Benjamin Strong was one of the most influential men during the FED's infancy. Strong was the head of the New York FED bank who understood elastic currency. He recognized that gold was no longer the only factor in controlling credit. In 1923

DON'T EAT DEBT

Strong stopped a recession by purchasing a large quantity of government securities. His aggressive action provided solid evidence that an open market operation was powerful enough to influence the availability of credit in the banking system. Strong was instrumental in elevating the solidity of the FED by establishing and promoting relationships with other central banks around the world. America was prospering. This time was deemed the "Era of Get Rich Quick", but everyone did not feel that way.

Rep. Carter Glass attempted to warn Congress that stock market speculation could lead to dire consequence. It was a lack of preemptive actions that led to the stock market crash of 1929. Before President-elect Hoover's inauguration he urged the Federal Reserve to curtail the public "risky and extreme" gambling on Wall Street. The FED raised the discount rate. The discount rate is the interest rate the FED charges when lending money to commercial banks. Raising the interest rate usually caused banks to borrow less money from the FED leaving them less money to lend to their customers. The FED attempted to detour the flow of speculative credit, but some bankers defied the government, bypassed the FED's discount window and offered banks $100 million in fresh loans to continue the stock market growth.

THE GREAT DEPRESSION: AMERICA'S SOUR SOUP

Even President Hoover admitted he did not use every tool available at his disposal to avoid the crash. He'd given a stock tip to a close friend before his investment took a nosedive. Today we would call his actions insider trading but that took place before the Securities and Exchange Commission was established. Wall Street's house of cards crashed. America entered the great depression. Despite the FED s attempt to slow speculative lending and slow the aggressive stock market growth people blamed the FED for failing to take appropriate action. It was believed that the FED failed to take more influential actions due to a lack of understanding of economics. Nearly 10,000 banks failed from 1930 to 1933.

Newly elected President Franklin D. Roosevelt inherited the biggest financial crisis in America's history. It was the words of his powerful inaugural speech that is constantly being repeated during the 2008 crisis. Let me give you a quote from that speech we as Americans need to embrace as we navigate through the crisis:

"This great nation will endure as it has endured, will revive and will prosper. So first of all let me assert my firm belief that the only thing we have to fear. . .is fear itself. . . nameless, unreasoning, unjustified terror which paralyzes needed efforts to convert retreat into advance."

It's the great Americans of our past that should inspire our perseverance to insure America's continued success. We must be aware of our past issues and obstacles that we as a nation have overcome to lead us to a hope and a brighter future. This book is a tool written to advance America's prosperity. During the Great Depression the U.S. government passed a host of legislations not only to help the economy to recover, but also to ensure that we never get into a depression like the one President Roosevelt inherited.

Shortly after FDR took office the FED became subordinate to the Executive Branch. Rep. Carter Glass sponsored a bill in reaction to factors that lead to the Great Depression. The Glass-

DON'T EAT DEBT

Steagall Act created the separation of Commercial and Investment banks and required that government securities be used as collateral for Federal Reserve's Notes. Remember that before this Glass-Steagall Act, gold was the collateral for each note printed. The government also standardized notes (Fiat notes/dollars) and reduced their size by thirty percent. Each denomination was redesigned to a standard format to decrease the different designs of various denominations in circulations making it easier for the public to distinguish counterfeit bills from the real legal tender. We were still on the gold standard, but the government loosed the gold to dollar ratio for dollars in circulation. When America went from gold or silver certificates to Federal Reserve Notes we did not fully leave the Gold standard. We decreased the quantity of gold required per printed or minted currency in circulation. We did not completely get off of the gold standard until 1974.

The Glass-Steagall Act furthermore created Federal Deposit Insurance Corporation (FDIC) and tasked them with being a watch dog over holding companies and open markets operation under the FED. As America was moving its monetary policies towards the FED, President Roosevelt recalled all gold and silver certificates making government securities the standard backing for American fiat money. If you look at the top of any monetary denomination from a one dollar to one hundred dollar bill between the numerical value of the bills you will see the words Federal Reserve Note. Prior to President Roosevelt's recall the statement read Silver or Gold Certificate. All federal currency issued since 1861 is still valid and redeemable for full face value.

CARLTON L RILEY SR

WHY WAS THE SOUP SOUR: SPECULATION

One of the major factors leading to the stock market crash of 1929 was stock market speculations. With speculation of endless stock growth, banks became over exuberant in stock market investments. At the time commercial banks handled both personal and investment accounts.

Before the great depression, most banks used patron's deposits to make investments. The bankers also encouraged clients to invest in the companies to which they (banks) funded. When the market crashed the banks that were heavily invested in the stock market became unstable, lost money and did not have the resources to cover all of their patron's accounts which caused most of these banks to fail.

The Glass-Steagall Act created a barrier between commercial and investment banks to prevent a loss of commercial deposits by non-investing clients in the event of investment accounts failure. Banks were given a year to decide whether they would specialize in Commercial or Investment banking.

Congress used the Securities Exchange Act of 1934 to create the Securities Exchange Commission. The SEC was created to regulate the unregulated stock market which was considered the main cause of the crash. Prior to 1929 investors had no way of determining the true value (if any) of the securities they were buying. The SEC estimated that nearly $25 million dollars of new securities purchased within a decade of the crash were deemed worthless. The SEC was created to restore investor confidence in the Stock Markets.

President Roosevelt named Joseph P. Kennedy the father of President John F. Kennedy to be the first chairman of the Securities Exchange Commission. The SEC was given the

DON'T EAT DEBT

authority over every aspects of the securities industry including register, regulate, and oversee brokerage firms, transfer agents and clearing agencies. The American Stock Exchange, New York Stock Exchange, National Association of Securities Dealers, which operates the NASDAQ are all regulated by the SEC. When Commercial and Investments banks were separated the SEC gained the responsibility of regulating Investment banks. Just as a reminder the Federal Reserve regulates Commercial banks.

Also in 1934 the Federal Credit Union Act was signed into law by President Roosevelt in an effort to make credit available and promote prudence through a national system of nonprofit banking. He authorizes the formation of federally chartered credit unions in all states. Initially NCUA was regulated by the Federal Deposit Insurance Corporation (FDIC) but shifted to the Federal Security Agency, and then the Department of Health, Education and Welfare. The National Credit Union Share Insurance Fund (NCUSIF) is the equivalent of the FDIC for other Commercial banks providing financial protections for its members. Unlike the FDIC the National Credit Union Share Insurance Fund (NCUSIF) was also formed to insure credit union deposits and NCUSIF was created without tax dollars and capitalized solely by credit unions.

Let's fast forward past the plethora of change in our monetary system to the 1970's when America was facing double digit inflation. During the recessions of the late seventies Paul Volker was sworn in Chairman of the FED. With his strong leadership and knowledge of monetary policies he successfully brought the overall double-digit inflation under control. During Mr. Volkers stead as Chairman, the Monetary Control Act of 1980 was passed. It required the FED to provide competitive prices for its financial services so that banks could compete against them for business. The act also required the FED to establish reserve requirements for all eligible financial institutions.

How Our Goose Got Cooked

One final bit of history I feel is absolutely necessary to include in the chapter. If the Glass-Steagall Act of 1933 was a goose then the Gramm-Leach-Bailey Act passed in 1999 would be the oven. Remember Glass-Steagall Act of 1933 was created after the 1929 stock market crash. Its objective was to prevent risky Investment banks which played a large role in the 1929 stock market crash from taking Commercial bank funding down with it.

Basically the Gramm-Leach-Bailey Act overturned the Glass-Steagall Act allowing banks to offer a menu of financial services, including commercial banking, investment banking and insurance sales all by the same American financial institution.

The "logical reasoning" Politian's used to argue merit for the Gramm-Leach-Bailey Act was the belief that it would allow financial institutions to operate as both investment and commercial bank as a single entity. Their argument was the Glass-Steagall Act put American banks at a disadvantage with other international full service banks causing customers to bank outside the United States.

In retrospect, it was not the poor practices of the International Full Service banks that drove America into the great depression and great recession in the 1929 and 2008; it was the American

DON'T EAT DEBT

banking practices. More than 4000 FDIC banks have closed since the 2008 crisis began according to the FDIC website 11 Nov 2011 and banks are still closing.

The average American including myself slept right through the passing of the Gramm-Leach-Bailey Act. We were totally oblivious to the future effects meaning the current economic issues Gramm-Leach-Bailey created. How ironic that this nation has seen its share of financial ups and downs since the great depression, but it was not until after the Gramm-Leach-Bailey Act that we reached the second worst financial crisis in America's young history. Just as it happened with the great depression so is it happening, other countries are entering into a recession of their own using the winning combined efforts of the full service banks. I said it in the beginning of this chapter and feel it is worth repeating, "Those who do not learn from history are doomed to repeat it". That is just food for thought!

CARLTON L RILEY SR

DON'T EAT DEBT

Chapter 6

Recipe for a Healthy Personal Economy

"There is an element in the readjustment of our financial system more important than currency, more important than gold, and that is the confidence of the people."
Franklin D. Roosevelt

The 2008 crisis was created by multiple issues intertwined together much like the ingredients in a sausage. As long as the job market was strong, consumer spending was up and credits markets flowed freely our economy was great. When fuel prices rose, consumer mortgages defaulted, and the credit market dried up leaving consumers afraid to spend, and then bam! We landed in a recession.

That's a simple view of our mess, but it is the way mortgages in mortgaged backed securities are securitized and cut into

DON'T EAT DEBT

tranches which reminds me most of sausages. No, I'm not hungry and everything does not remind me of food, but it is the easiest analogy I could use to create a simple image of a complex issue. When all of the ingredients come together they produce a product which depending on how much debt you consumed will determine if you are emotionally full from over borrowing and sickened by the idea we're using our tax dollars to bailout a few greedy Americans. Either way the process left America and rest of the world in a recession.

It should be comforting to you that you now know and understand more about the crisis then you did prior to picking up this book. If you were better informed about the FED and monetary history you would have been better prepared for the crisis.

The opportunities to purchase MBS and CDS has not passed, these products are still available. Oddly enough you can even purchase MBS for cars. They have lost most of the alluring shine they once had. Now that we know to remain vigilant of investment bubbles growing in our economy, we must be more vigilant, watch for signs and respond accordingly. Look for signs of weakness or over confidence in the markets over a prolonged period of time. It could be a sign of an economic bubble forming. By bubble I'm referring to a focused growth in a specific market. You can recognize a bubble when the media speaks of its unrelenting growth as if it is rising with no decline in sight. Like the previous disasters such as the internet or real estate bubbles they all burst leaving severely damaged economies. Bubbles hurt the economy by drawing investors to specific market which causes them to not invest in commonly stable markets. A bubble is like a beautiful weed in the midst of your rose garden which may not appear to be a weed at first, but if not rooted out will steal all of the water and nutrition that should be going to your rose and cause it to die. Once the bubble burst or the weed is rooted out the investor's money or water and nutrition flows back to needed source restoring its original health or glory. We need to apply the lessons learned from this crisis. If you notice a bubble forming start conversations with your circle of influence to call their attention to what you are seeing. If it is a clearly formed bubble contact your government representation to put tools in place to make sure we don't keep recycling the same ingredients for failure. If all else fails brace yourself and family for the crash to come when the next bubble bursts.

I truly believe the repeal of the Glass-Steagall Act of 1933 played a major part of the 2008 crisis. That is not to say that real estate market would not have clasped, but I believe it would not had such a lasting effect on the banks. We elect political officials to work on our behalf but we have to monitor what they are doing for the good of their constituents namely we the citizens.

For all it's worth the government can't untangle the mortgaged sausages. In 2008 we were served Mortgage backed sausages a la mode for our financial lunch and we have eaten so much we have become economically sick. By eaten I'm referring to the crisis eating up our tax dollars which could have been used to lower our debt.

Now the securitized mortgages mix (CDO, MBS) are fully cooked so the only thing we can do is eat this American made product cold. Cold because little was done to banks officials

DON'T EAT DEBT

who created the risky investments and kept all of the profits, so they were never in any real hot water with government regulator. They only received a slap on the wrist while we bailed them out and they continued to eat steak and lobster.

You know the old saying, no pain no gain and the fees changed against the financial institutions are inadequate to inflict any real pain against their fiscal irresponsibility. Consider this book the cold cup of water to wash down the cold nasty recovery meal.

By now you should know enough of the economist language to help make some sense of the media rhetoric. Hopefully you now understand what the FED, SEC, AIG acronyms stand for and what these organizations do. In addition to organization acronym, I covered product acronyms such as the meaning of MBS, CDO and CMO to name a few. I have given you a brief history of the American financial system so you know our system is not perfect by far but it's a work in progress. For the remainder of this and the last two chapters we will look at the role the President, FED and the Secretary of the Treasury play in the recovery process. Every American should know this information going forward so that you can be a watchman over the nation's economy.

If you see an enemy approaching our gates to do economic harm, make sure you sound the alarm by telling everyone of the impending invaders plans and how they can potentially hurt our national economy.

Please tell your friends, co-workers and anyone that will listen. Call your congressional or government representative from the local level to as high as you can go until they invoke changes.

CARLTON L RILEY SR

Purposely watch and read media sources to see what is happening in the world of finance. Pay attention to who's speaking when they are talking about the US economy. When you hear Politicians talking about the "recession" or the economy in general pay close attention to understand what factors they are using to measure and justify their statements.

THE PRESIDENT

The President is the primary and most important American whom you need to pay close attention to concerning the American economy. He was voted into office to oversee America's continual presence as a beacon of hope for the world and to maintain the health of our nation. His voice is not the only one we should focus on for the direction of our economy. In the eighties there was a commercial which said, "When EF Hutton speaks everyone listens." Well truthfully that same sentiment should be said about the current Chairman of the Federal Reserve.

In the history chapter we gave an introduction to the Federal Reserve System. The Federal Reserve is an independent governmental entity being a part of the Government, yet does not have to gain permission from any of our governing branches to make monetary decisions. The chairman of the FED reports to Congress on the Federal Reserve monetary policy objectives at a minimum of twice per year. The current chairman's name is Ben Bernanke. The Chairman also testifies before Congress on numerous other issues (especially when the economy is doing badly or emergency arises). He also meets with the Secretary of the Treasury. At its initial creation the Treasury department oversaw the Federal Reserve operations.

DON'T EAT DEBT

The FED oversees America's monetary policy but the Treasury oversees America's Fiscal policies. What is the difference you ask? The difference is monetary policy (managed by the FED) primarily deals with the availability and cost of money and credit to help promote our national economic goals.

Fiscal policy (managed by the Treasury Department) focuses on policies that affect tax rates and government spending in an effort to control the economy. The Treasury also oversees the production of coins and currency, the disbursement of payments to the public, revenue collection via the Internal Revenue Service, and the funds to run the federal government.

The Secretary of the Treasury is a presidential cabinet position selected by the President and confirmed by the Senate. The Chairman and Vice Chairman of the Federal Reserve are also appointed by the President and confirmed by the Senate.

The nominees for the Federal Reserve must already be one of the ten members on the Board or must be simultaneously appointed to the Board. The terms for these positions are four years. The Board's responsibilities include a thorough analysis of domestic and international financial and economic developments.

But rest assured if these officials including chairmen for one of the Federal Reserve branch offices are speaking pay close attention to what they are saying and doing. They affect every incoming and outgoing American dollar.

CARLTON L RILEY SR

DON'T EAT DEBT

CHAPTER 7

A HUNGRY NATION MUST BE FED

"GIVE ME CONTROL OF A NATION'S MONEY AND I CARE NOT WHO MAKES HER LAWS." MAYER AMSCHEL ROTHSCHILD

December 23, 1913 President Woodrow Wilson signed the Federal Reserve Act into law establishing the Federal Reserve System as America answers the nations cry to stabilize, organize and standardize the banking system. It has been our central bank for nearly 100 years.

The FED is a decentralized central banking system ran by both government elected officials and non-governmental employees. The concept of the Federal Reserve has remained the same but its role is not the same. Today the role of the Federal Reserve has changed. The purpose of the FED is to:

- Hold the banking reserves of the United States and discount paper for their member banks.

DON'T EAT DEBT

- They also provide financial services to the U.S. government, U.S. financial institutions, and foreign official institutions.

- They issue and redeem the principal currency of the country and distribute the metallic money coined by the mints.

- They collect checks and practically all other types of instruments of payment for their members.

- They effect settlements of domestic exchanges.

- Fiscal agents of the Treasury operations: Government debt, receives deposit of revenues, and pay checks drawn by the disbursing offices.

Now the FED does not work for free and charges for all of the functions listed above. The FED is not a branch of the US Government. The Federal Reserve System is an independent entity within our government. The FED gets its authority from the Federal Reserve Act of 1913 and Congress.

As an independent entity of the government, their decisions DO NOT have to be ratified by anyone in either the legislative branch or the executive including the President. Because they are considered a not-for-profit organization they use the money gained for services to cover operating costs making it a self-sustaining organization. Any money the FED receives above operation cost is given to the treasury department for government use. It was set up that way so that it would be free from political influences. It insures the FED makes decision for the good of the country not for the good of a political group or politician re-election campaign.

CARLTON L RILEY SR

THREE HELPINGS OF FED PIE

The FED uses three tools to regulate the American economy. It uses the discount rate, the reserve requirement and open market operations. To help the FED with the business of regulating the economy the Banking Act of 1935 was passed creating the Federal Open Market Committee (FOMC) as a permanent legal entity. The FOMC works on formulation and conduct of monetary policy for the U.S. economy. They meet eight times per year to set key interest rates referring to the discount rate.

ONE SLICE OF PIE IS THE DISCOUNT WINDOW

The discount rate is the interest rate charged to commercial banks by the Federal Reserve Bank's lending facility. The practice of lending to these depository institutions is referred to as the discount window. The discount window offers three fully secured type loans which are: seasonal credit, secondary credit, and primary credit, each with its own interest rate.

Seasonal credit is issued to depository in agricultural or seasonal resort communities most of which are small banks. The reason for seasonal credit is due to recurring intra-year fluctuations in funds needed i.e. harvesting, planting or vacation/holiday business needs.

Secondary credit is generally used to resolve severe financial difficulties or to meet short-term liquidity needs.

Primary credit loans are extended under generally sound financial conditions for a very short term usually overnight. Not all banks qualify for the primary credit at the discount window and thus need to resort to secondary or seasonal loans from the FED.

DON'T EAT DEBT

Think of the FED as the banker's bank. Make sure you pay close attention when the chairman of the FED speaks. As a side note pay attention when any of the FED Governors speak because they are always focused on money (nationally and internationally) and know what is going on.

When you tune into a news report and the chairman of the FED says he is raising the interest rate, he is referring to the interest rates the FED charges banks for primary loans.

Here is the principle theory for why the FED lowers interest rate on loans: if they lower the interest rates to their customers then the banks will offer lower (although higher than their FED rate) to customers. The borrowers will use it to either boost productive in their business or purchase big ticketed items increasing demand for goods and services thus improving the economy.

The FED uses the discount window to regulate the economy. If the FED wanted to slow the economic growth they raise interest rates causing banks to borrow less money from the FED thus banks loan less money to their customers and slow the economy. These efforts are done to control inflation.

We the people have to pay close attention to what's going on in the economy. Your understanding of this tool could be the difference between paying 3% interest on the pickup truck loan when the discount rate is low and 6% more on the same loan caused by the lack of attention when the chairman of the FED said he would raise the discount rate to slow the economy.

Here is another example of the use of this Federal Reserve discount window. I will restate it to make sure it's clear. If the Chairman says he is going to lower interest rates, he is not referring to the personal interest rates you are currently paying on your bank loans unless you have an adjustable rate mortgage. When the chairman says he is going to lower interest rates he is referring to the discount rate. The discount rate is the interest rate the FED charges financial institutions for short-term reserve loans. The Federal Reserve is the Bankers bank. If banks borrow money from the FED and get a lower interest rate then the banks are more likely to lend more money to customer with a lower interest. The customer borrows more money to help them grow their business. People who make money tend to spend more money. When more money is available, people tend to spend more on goods and services. Demand is created when we spend more money on goods and service which cause production to increase. The lowering of unemployment levels is a sign of a healthy rebounding economy. As companies strive to keep up with demand it brings about an increase in American dollars in circulation.

This is an example of the law of supply and demand in effect. The dollar increases in value when America's currency in continual circulation which is how the dollar gets it value. The more money in circulation means more taxes being generated for governmental operation and expenses. If the economy is healthy meaning growing while keeping inflation levels low, the government sells fewer treasury bonds and usually begin to buy back bonds which in turn lowers our deficit. If Americans put more money into savings while still making some purchases it would drastically change our economy for the good and also have a positive impact on the deficit. The buying and selling of the bonds is a 24 hour operation which most citizens are unaware it is even taking place but never the less, the FED monitors the money to bonds ratio to regulate the economy. We will talk more about that in the next section. So if you hear

DON'T EAT DEBT

the discount window is open listen to the reason why it is open and make your financial plan accordingly.

SECOND SLICE OF PIE IS OPEN MARKET OPERATIONS

Another tool in the FED arsenal is the open market operations. Open market operation is when the Federal Reserve purchases and sells U.S. Treasury and federal agency securities on the open market to influence short-term interest rates and the growth of money and credit. Policy regarding open market operations is established by the FOMC which is a part of the Federal Reserve. Again the FOMC (Federal Open Market Committee) works on formulation and conduct of monetary policy for the U.S. economy.

In order to expand or contract the amount of money in the banking system, the Federal Open Market Committee buys and sells Treasury Bonds.

By purchasing Treasury Bonds, Bills and Notes they can inject money into the banking system and stimulate growth. Sales of the securities do the opposite. When the FED buys back securities it is in essence buying back our debt, which makes the dollar stronger because we owe less money to investors. So when you hear the dollar is strong that means we are selling less debt in the form of Treasury Bonds, Bills and Notes. If we're standing still or purchasing debt back, both are better than selling financial instruments.

When America has to sell securities it means the nation is not generating enough revenue to pay our debt thus we must borrow money from another country to cover our obligations and repay them with interest. The more debt we sell the higher risk the buyer of the bond takes for fear we may one day not be able to pay them back. Higher risk means the buyer has a greater chance of negotiating the terms of the bond (i.e. interest rates and repay periods) and since we need the money we must comply. Just to make it clear, if you hear the Chairman buying US treasury bonds, then he's saying to you that American's are saving money so we don't need to borrow from another country. The chairman's actions may also mean the economy growing so fast it may spark inflationary growth so the FED has to spend money buying back bonds to leave fewer dollars to lend banks through the discount window. Regardless of the actions taken by the chairman of the FED Wall Street always pays close attention because his words could be the difference between making and losing money. The FED chairman affects your money as well.

Third slice of Fed pie is the Reserve Requirement

The third tool the FED uses to control America's economy is the Reserve requirement. The FED determines how much money a financial institution has to deposit in the regional Federal Reserve Bank in case of an emergency.

The remaining money received from deposits by customers is considered created money. Banks use the remaining portion to loans to patrons (with interest of course) which means they don't need to borrow money from the FED to increase their bottom line. This process is called fractional reserve banking.

The FED tells the bank to maintain a percentage of reserves (of cash and coin or deposits at the central bank) which is called the reserve ratio. The bank charges you fees to hold and perform transactions on your account. They will pay you interest on your money in savings (nowhere near the interest they charge borrowers) but they will make money loaning your

DON'T EAT DEBT

money to someone else charging them a higher interest rate then they pay you making them richer. If the FED raises the reserve ratio then banks have less to lend slowing the money in circulation which in turns slows the economy. If the FED lowers the reserve ratio then banks have money to lend putting more money into circulation speeding up the economy providing room for the economy to grow.

THE FEDERAL RESERVE: WHERE BANKERS DINE

I mentioned in the introduction about my lack of understanding how personal checks are processed. ACH (which means automatic clearing house) is a modern day function of the clearinghouse discussed in *chapter 5 section titled Lets Cook*. Today various forms of transactions from paper checks to electronic credits converge to one location to exchange notes for credits from one account to another by the Federal Reserve. In his book *The Age of Turbulence*, Alan Greenspan said the Federal Reserve is in charge of the electronic payment systems that transfer more than $4 trillion dollars a day in money and securities between banks all over the country and much of the world.

How does it work? When you present a paper check the receiving institution keys in pertinent information from the check or scans the check into a computer and makes the appropriate entries on its books. They debit the check writer's account and credit the depositor's account. The scanned check's image or keyed information is transmitted directly to the paying bank. The check receiving institution forwards the paper checks or images of the checks to a correspondent for collection, exchanges checks, in paper or electronic form, with a group of banks participating in a clearinghouse arrangement, or forwards the paper checks or images of the checks to a Federal Reserve Bank for collection. The Federal Reserve Banks charge depositors a fee for check-clearing services. The check clearing process has become so streamlined until some check receiving locations can process a check quicker than a credit card purchase. For some American's this is bad news. If any of you in the past have ever written a check hoping for the 3 day processing time these days are quickly diminishing. Some establishment processing time vary because they can only get immediate or real time processing during normal FED operations and then after hours have to delay processing until the next business day. Remember it's not paper currency being used just electronic credits and debits. Banks still pay the FED a processing fee even if the check is returned. This is a basic explanation of how check processing works and an example of one of the tasks assigned to the Federal Reserve.

SECRETARY OF TREASURY

Always pay close attention to the Secretary of Treasury. In the history chapter we stated that the FED is the government's bank. When the economy slows down or worse goes into a recession or depression, then the President working with the Secretary of Treasury and Congress are tasked with getting the economy back on track through fiscal policies.

Politicians are often pointing fingers blaming each other's political parties for not fixing the economy but if the politicians aren't part of the solution then they are part of the problem. The government writes bills and proposals to spend our tax dollars to get things moving in the right direction. It was Congress working with the President who approved the bailout dollars in an attempt to get the economy back on track or ever

DON'T EAT DEBT

slow its deterioration. As we continue to recover from the crisis pay attention to is:

- Where your tax dollars are being spent?
- What accountability processes are in place to insure proper use of the funds?
- What additional spending (earmarks) is being added to proposals that are not necessarily going to help the economy?

I said government is spending our tax dollars, but I must clarify. Some if not most of the money being spent today is based on projected future revenue. We are using current revenue collected from current taxpayers to pay interest on treasury securities. Also do your homework after each election or Treasury Secretary appointment to see their past organization. The Treasury Secretary has to be a great communicator and real go-getter or else the President won't be able to get any budget and monetary goals accomplished. As we continue the trend of borrowing to spend we eat away at GDP and GDP determines tax dollars. Just like the "continental" was depended on potential tax revenue collected from the developing nation, present day America is so deep in debt right now it will take critical spending reforms to get our debt under control to avoid deflation of the dollar.

As our elected officials strive to get us out of the recession, there are some pros to the correction in the market place. I'm sure you have experienced at some point in your life the prices on goods and services dropping from fuel to toilet paper. When the economy stops shrinking banks start lending and issuing credit spurning consumer spending. Strong companies press forward and new companies continually arise from the rubble with strength, resilience and fortitude. Once again our nation demonstrates how the free market system keeps American Spirit alive!

WATCH THE POT

It is said a watched pot never boils so if we stay actively vigilant we may be able to prevent the greedy endeavors of the few from boiling over into our troubled economy. Watch the stock market even if you are not an investor. It's usually an indication of the nation's economic health. Often times you will hear financial commentators referring to the stock market as a bull or bear market, these terms are metaphors for the movement of the market. When you hear the term bull market it refers to the way a bull thrusts its horns up into the air when it attacks an opponent. So in a bull market stocks are going up and the economy is growing.

The term bear market refers to the way a bear swipes its paws downward when it attacks an opponent. In a bear market stock sales are slowing down and investors are buying fewer stocks. When stocks sales begin to decrease due to a bear market, then most investors start buying bonds. In a bear market the economy is still growing financially, just at a slower pace. One other warning concerning a bull and bear market as it relates to the business cycle. At one phase of the business cycle there is a correction in the market so spending slows downs. The correction should not be mistaken as a bear market.

We've fallen, but we will get up. It is in our diversity of people, personalities and cultures that cause visitors to come from around the world to behold our greatness. The same hope that rests upon the hearts of the original colonists still resides upon

DON'T EAT DEBT

every American heart today which is we are only limited to our willingness to achieve greatness in this nation and we refuse to settle for mediocrity.

CHAPTER 8

WILL THAT BE CASH OR CREDIT

"I AM NOT WORRIED ABOUT THE DEFICIT. IT IS BIG ENOUGH TO TAKE CARE OF ITSELF." RONALD REAGAN

"We the people of the United States, in order to form a more perfect union, establish justice, insure domestic tranquility, provide for the common defense, promote the general welfare, and secure the blessings of liberty to ourselves and our posterity, do ordain and establish this Constitution for the United States of America."

These words have been forgotten by most Americans. When was the last time you thought about them and what do they mean to you? I've taken the liberty of adding definition to a few words which will provide a deeper understanding which I hope will help you re-fire your God given rights as an American.

DON'T EAT DEBT

"We the people of the United States, in order to form a more perfect union, establish justice, insure meaning to make certain especially by taking necessary measures and precautions domestic tranquility free from disturbance or turmoil, provide for the common defense, promote or furthering the progress of the general welfare being health, happiness, and fortunes of a person or group, and secure the blessings of liberty to ourselves and our posterity for all future generations, do ordain to establish or order by appointment, decree, or law and establish to institute as a law permanently by enactment or agreement this Constitution an established law or custom for the United States of America."

How did we manage to get so far away from the basic premise of the first sentence of the American constitution? We no longer erupt in outrage at the selfish actions of greedy rich Americans. Lack of understanding of the decisions of lawmakers influenced by lobbyists has once again proven the accuracy of Benjamin Franklin's words, "The only thing more expensive than education is ignorance." American debt is sixteen trillion dollars and rising with no real end in sight. We, the average citizens such as you and I have to be more proactive in reversing the deficit. It's not just our right as sovereign citizens but our duty to preserve a more perfect union for future generations. We must pay attention to the actions of the Federal Reserve as they bear a direct relationship to every dollar in America.

AMERICA'S DEBT: THE HEARTBURN AFTER THE MEAL

In the previous chapter we talked about the Federal Open Market Committee work to formulate and establish monetary policy for the U.S. economy. Through the control of buying and selling of Treasury instruments the FOMC can either expand or contract the amount of money in the banking system.

Deficit spending is when the government spends more money than the nation generates through taxes and other sources of income. The difference between government revenues and the unfunded budget is made up by borrowing through the issuance of debt (government bonds) which is why we have to sell Treasury Bonds, Bills and Notes to cover our shortages and help the dollar maintain its value. If we lose buyers for our securities, the dollar will end up like the "continentals." Greece is continued economic troubles plague the news as it struggles to remain part of the European Union. Its economic troubles caused its bonds rating to drop making them a high credit risk to buyers. Eventually if they run out of buyers for their bonds or fail to keep agreements with the European Central bank the country could go into bankruptcy. Its fate that I pray America avoids.

In my forty plus years of life I've come to the understanding that in a recession there is never a shortage of money in the world; it is just a matter of knowing where to find it then secure a portion for yourself. We as a nation need to get back to being more economically reliant upon ourselves. In 1980 Americans saved 10% of their income. For America that meant banks with customer's money in the form of saving deposits in their vaults don't have to borrow money from the FED to make personal and business loans to customers. With banks needing to borrow less money from the FED; the FED is free to buy back bonds from the holders which strengthens the dollar. Today we save less than 1% leaving every non-saving American partially responsible for our growing deficit.

Below is a chart which shows why various media sources say China owns America. As of June 2012 mainland China is the

DON'T EAT DEBT

single largest foreign purchaser of T-Notes, bonds and bills followed by Japan. China owns $1164.3 billion dollars of America's note with Japan owning $1119.3 billion.

If they ever attempt to redeem them all at once, America may possibly default as a nation but I pray not. We must pass this message on before it is too late. In the chart below you can see the percentages of Treasury Securities held by major foreign countries and local American groups.

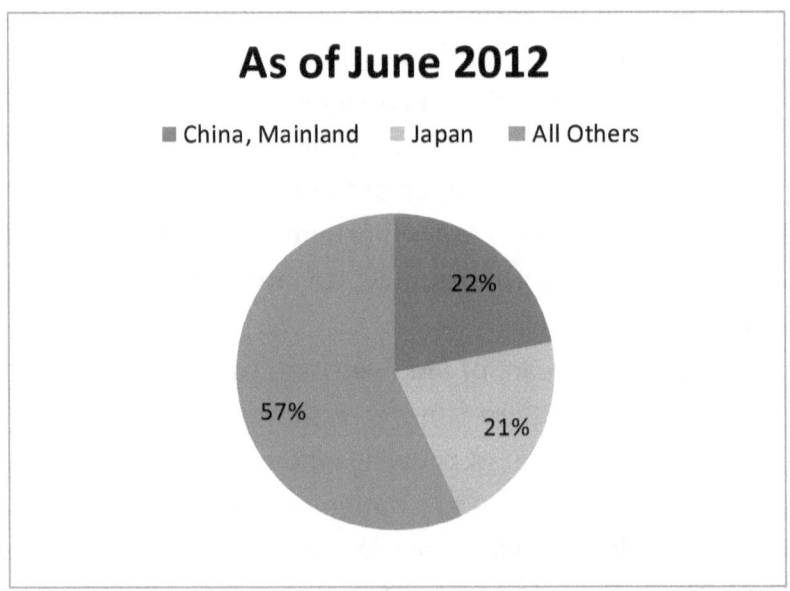

- This chart represents our largest two foreign contributors
- All others include purchasers from 35 other countries
- To check for an up to date record of the holders of the U.S. debt go to http://www.treasury.gov/resource-center/data-chart-center/tic/Documents/mfh.txt

CARLTON L RILEY SR

For me changes for a better economy started when I wrote this book and it started with you purchasing a copy for yourself and a few copies for others to read and take action. Together we can use the power we hold as American citizens to save our nation from this debt dilemma.

THE AFTER DINNER MINT

According to the Bureau of Public Debt the U.S. has been in debt since we became a nation, but only if you don't include the actions of President Andrew Jackson whom out of anger removed all federal funds from the 2nd bank of the United States and placed it in a state owned bank.

Although politicians continue to spend more money than we generate through taxes, the nation's public debt has a pattern of expediential growing during war times. Debt incurred during the American Revolutionary war amounted to $75,463,476.52 not including the debt created as the cost of building a nation. Not a bad price to give birth to a nation.

The cost of Independence:

Boston Tea Party (estimated cost of Tea)   10,000 British pounds

Fighting a war of independence
$75,463,476.52

Creating the greatest nation on earth
PRICELESS

It was Alexander Hamilton who said, "The United States debt, foreign and domestic, was the price of Liberty." The national debt grew from $65 million in 1860 to $2.7 billion after the

DON'T EAT DEBT

American Civil war. It grew to approximately $22 billion after World War I and $260 billion after World War II. For several decades following WWII the national or public debt grew nearly at the same rate of inflation until the 1980's when it began to grow exponentially. The national debt more than tripled from 1980 to 1990; by 2008 our national debt was 10.3 trillion.

We have to take effective steps to decrease our national debt. You are already moving in the right direction by reading this book. Education, planning and implementation of viable plans are the only ways we will truly be able to find financial peace as a nation. Make sure you continue your financial education once you finish this book. More information can be found on the Bureau of Public Debt website:

http://www.publicdebt.treas.gov/index.htm

In an effort to limit the U.S debt Congress granted the Treasury authority to issue as much debt as needed to fund government operations as long as the total debt did not exceed a stated "debt ceiling". As of February 2009 the debt limit was raised to over $12 trillion dollars. As I finish this book in November 2012 the debt is now up to $16 trillion. If you are fed up with the way things are going please increase your efforts to keep America the most prosperous nation on the Planet.

CARLTON L RILEY SR

APPENDEX

CARLTON L RILEY SR

FEDERAL RESERVES BANKS

Atlanta
1000 Peachtree Street NE
Atlanta, GA 30309

(404) 498-8500

Boston
600 Atlantic Avenue
Boston, MA 02210
(617) 973-3000

Cleveland
1455 East Sixth Street
Cleveland, OH 44114
(216) 579-2000

Chicago
230 South LaSalle Street
Chicago, IL 60604

(312) 322-5322

Dallas
2200 North Pearl Street
Dallas, TX 75201
(214) 922-6000

Kansas City
1 Memorial Drive
Kansas City, MO 64198
(816) 881-2000

Minneapolis
90 Hennepin Avenue
Minneapolis, MN 55401
(612) 204-5000

New York
33 Liberty Street
New York, NY 10045
(212) 720-5000

Philadelphia
Ten Independence Mall
Philadelphia, PA 19106
(215) 574-6000

Richmond
701 East Byrd Street
Richmond, VA 23219
(804) 697-8000

St. Louis
One Federal Reserve Bank Plaza
Broadway and Locust Streets
St. Louis, MO 63102
(314) 444-8444

San Francisco
101 Market Street
San Francisco, CA 94105
(415) 974-2000

DON'T EAT DEBT

The System serves commonwealths and territories as follows:

- New York Bank serves: Commonwealth of Puerto Rico; U.S. Virgin Islands

- San Francisco Bank serves: American Samoa; Guan; Commonwealth of the Northern Mariana Islands; Hawaii

- Seattle Branch serves: Alaska

CARLTON L RILEY SR

The following pages can be found on :

http://www.frbsf.org/publications/federalreserve/annual/1995/history.html#A8

DON'T EAT DEBT

This is a pictured an extremely rare silver certificate, series of 1878, payable at New York. The head is of James Monroe.

This is an extremely rare note known as a "Grand Watermelon" note because of the shape of the zeroes. It was redeemable in coin, and it has Rosecrans-Huston signatures and a large brown seal. The head is of General George Gordon Meade, commander of the Union troops at the battle of Gettysburg.

DON'T EAT DEBT

This is a copy of legal ten thousand dollar bill used by Federal Reserve Bank partners transferring funds between banks.

This is a picture of a National Bank note. This note was issued from 1919 to 1921, only in Ohio and Louisiana.

DON'T EAT DEBT

NOTES

CARLTON L RILEY SR

DON'T EAT DEBT

Carlton L. Riley Sr. is a former assistant Intelligence Analyst for the United States Army. He also served as an Electronic Commerce Analyst at CSX Railroad, and Senior Quality Analyst for SourceOne Healthcare Technologies, a leading imaging equipment company, radiographic supplies and services. He currently resides in Jacksonville, Florida with his wife and four children.

www.ingramcontent.com/pod-product-compliance
Lightning Source LLC
Chambersburg PA
CBHW030820180526
45163CB00003B/1361